Martin Luther King, Jr.
1929–1968

An *EBONY* Picture Biography

Revised Edition 2007

Johnson Publishing Company, Inc.

Library of Congress Cataloging-in-Publication Data

Martin Luther King, Jr., 1929–1968.—Rev. ed.
p. cm.
"An *EBONY* Picture Biography."
ISBN: 978-0-87485-005-5
1. King, Martin Luther, Jr., 1929-1968—Pictorial works. 2. African Americans—Biography—Pictorial works.
3. Civil rights workers—United States--Biography—Pictorial works. 4. Baptists—United States—Clergy—
Biography—Pictorial works. 5. African Americans—Civil rights—History—20th century—Pictorial works.
6. Civil rights movements—United States—History—20th century—Pictorial works.
E185.97.K5M3 2007
323.092—dc22
[B]   2007023332

www.jpcbooks.com

Photographs by:

Richard Anderson, Associated Press, Lacey Crawford, Detroit News, Frederick Douglas Devan, Jack Finley, Bob Fitch,
Arthur L. Freeman, Bill Gillohm, Norman L. Hunter, International News, Ed Jackson, Roy Lewis, Henry Martin,
Kenneth Moore, Morehouse College, Harmon Perry, Rhoden's Photo Service, Charles Sanders, Howard Simmons,
Moneta Sleet, Jr., Maurice Sorrell, Isaac Sutton, John Tweedle, UPI, Wyatt T. Walker, Charles Walter, G. Marshall
Wilson, Hal A. Franklin, William Lanier, Jim Atkins and Robert Lackenbach.

Cover Photographs by Moneta Sleet, Jr.

FOREWORD

Martin Luther King, Jr., was born on January 15, 1929, at his family's home in Atlanta, Georgia. During his lifetime, Dr. King became an international symbol of the fight for human rights, and he was awarded the Nobel Peace Prize in 1964. His walks with kings and marches with poor people made him one of the most admired men in history. Dr. King was assassinated in Memphis, Tennessee, on April 4, 1968 at the age of 39.

At the time of Dr. King's death, there was emptiness in the hearts of his many supporters and admirers. Shortly thereafter, the editors of *Ebony* selected photos from the *Ebony* photo files that highlighted Dr. King's private and public lives and published them in this pictorial history.

Excerpts from Dr. King's most inspired speeches and writings have been included. They recapture the emotion and the significance of the historic moments pictured and include his prophetic "I've Been to the Mountaintop" sermon, delivered on April 3, 1968, in Memphis, Tennessee and his "Letter from a Birmingham Jail" written on April 18, 1963. Also, Dr. King's eulogy, which was delivered by his mentor, Dr. Benjamin E. Mays, introduces the book.

This revised edition encompasses his life as a husband and father, faithful pastor, great orator, and peace advocate who changed the world.

Dr. Benjamin E. Mays was president of Morehouse College in Atlanta, GA from 1940 to 1967. Considered Dr. King's "spiritual mentor" and "intellectual father," Dr. Mays advised the Nobel Laureate and other students who became doctors, lawyers, politicians, educators, and ministers.

Eulogy by Dr. Benjamin E. Mays
President Emeritus, Morehouse College

To be honored by being requested to give the eulogy at the funeral of Dr. Martin Luther King Jr. is like asking one to eulogize his deceased son — so close and so precious was he to me. Our friendship goes back to his student days at Morehouse. It is not an easy task; nevertheless I accept it, with a sad heart and with full knowledge of my inadequacy to do justice to this man. It was my desire that if I predeceased Dr. King, he would pay tribute to me on my final day. It was his wish that if he predeceased me, I would deliver the homily at his funeral. Fate has decreed that I eulogize him. I wish it might have been otherwise...

God called the grandson of a slave on his father's side, and the grandson of a man born during the Civil War on his mother's side, and said to him: Martin Luther, speak to America about war and peace; about social justice and racial discrimination; about its obligation to the poor; and about nonviolence as a way of perfecting social change in a world of brutality and war.

Let it be thoroughly understood that our deceased brother did not embrace nonviolence out of fear or cowardice. Moral courage was one of his noblest virtues. As Mahatma Gandhi challenged the British Empire without a sword and won, Martin Luther King Jr. challenged the interracial wrongs of his country without a gun. And he had the faith to believe that he would win the battle for social justice. I make bold to assert that it took more courage for

King to practice nonviolence than it took his assassin to fire the fatal shot. The assassin is a coward: He committed his dastardly deed and fled. When Martin Luther disobeyed an unjust law, he accepted the consequences of his actions. He never ran away and he never begged for mercy. He returned to the Birmingham jail to serve his time.

Perhaps he was more courageous than soldiers who fight and die on the battlefield. There is an element of compulsion in their dying. But when Martin Luther faced death again and again, and finally embraced it, there was no external pressure. He was acting on an inner compulsion that drove him on. More courageous than those who advocate violence as a way out, for they carry weapons of destruction for defense. But Martin Luther faced the dogs, the police, jail, heavy criticism, and finally death; and he never carried a gun, not even a knife to defend himself...

Coupled with moral courage was Martin Luther King Jr.'s capacity to love people. Though deeply committed to a program of freedom for Negroes, he had love and concern for all kinds of peoples. He drew no distinction between the high and low; none between the rich and the poor. He believed especially that he was sent to champion the cause of the man farthest down. He would probably say that if death had to come, I am sure there was no greater cause to die for than fighting to get a just wage for garbage collectors. He was supra-race, supra-nation, supra-denomination, supra-class and supra-culture. He belonged to the world and to mankind. Now he belongs to posterity.

But there is a dichotomy in all this. This man was loved by some and hated by others. If any man knew the meaning of suffering, King knew. House bombed; living day by day for 13 years under constant threats of death; maliciously accused of being a Communist; falsely accused of being insincere and seeking limelight for his own glory; stabbed by a member of his own race; slugged in a hotel lobby; jailed 30 times; occasionally deeply hurt because his friends betrayed him - and yet this man had no bitterness in his heart, no rancor in his soul, no revenge in his mind; and he went up and down the length and breadth of this world preaching nonviolence and the redemptive power of love. He believed with all of his heart, mind and soul that the way to peace and brotherhood is through nonviolence, love and suffering. He was severely criticized for his opposition to the war in Vietnam. It must be said, however, that one could hardly expect a prophet of Dr. King's commitments to advocate nonviolence at home and violence in Vietnam. Nonviolence to King was total commitment not only in solving the problems of race in the United States, but in solving the problems of the world.

Surely this man was called of God to do this work. If Amos and Micah were prophets in the eighth century B.C., Martin Luther King Jr. was a prophet in the 20th century…

Moneta Sleet's Pulitzer Prize-winning photo of Mrs. Coretta Scott King and her daughter Bernice at Dr. King's funeral.

If Jesus was called to preach the Gospel to the poor, Martin Luther was called to give dignity to the common man. If a prophet is one who interprets in clear and intelligible language the will of God, Martin Luther King Jr. fits that designation. If a prophet is one who does not seek popular causes to espouse, but rather the causes he thinks are right, Martin Luther qualified on that score.

…He was not ahead of his time. No man is ahead of his time. Every man is within his star, each in his time. Each man must respond to the call of God in his lifetime and not in somebody else's time. Jesus had to respond to the call of God in the first century A.D., and not in the 20th century. He had but one life to live. He couldn't wait. How long do you think Jesus would have had to wait for the constituted authorities to accept him? Twenty-five years? A hundred years? A thousand? He died at 33. He couldn't wait. Paul, Galileo, Copernicus, Martin Luther the Protestant reformer, Gandhi and Nehru couldn't wait for another time. They had to act in their lifetimes. No man is ahead of his time. Abraham, leaving his country in the obedience to God's call; Moses leading a rebellious people to the Promised Land; Jesus dying on a cross, Galileo on his knees recanting; Lincoln dying of an assassin's bullet; Woodrow Wilson crusading for a League of Nations; Martin Luther King Jr. dying fighting for justice for garbage collectors - none of these men were ahead of their time. With them the time was always ripe to do that which was right and that which needed to be done.

Too bad, you say, that Martin Luther King Jr. died so young. I feel that way, too. But, as I have said many times before, it isn't how long one lives, but how well. It's what one accomplishes for mankind that matters. Jesus died at 33; Joan of Arc at 19; Byron and Burns at 36; Keats at 25; Marlow at 29; Shelley at 30; Dunbar before 35; John Fitzgerald Kennedy at 46; William Rainey Harper at 49; and Martin Luther King Jr. at 39.

We all pray that the assassin will be apprehended and brought to justice. But, make no mistake, the American people are in part responsible for Martin Luther King Jr.'s death. The assassin heard enough condemnation of King and of Negroes to feel that he had public support. He knew that millions hated King…

If we love Martin Luther King Jr., and respect him, as this crowd surely testifies, let us see to it that he did not die in vain; let us see to it that we do not dishonor his name by trying to solve our problems through rioting in the streets. Violence was foreign to his nature. He

Dr. Benjamin E. Mays and Rev. Ralph D. Abernathy, two of Dr. King's closest advisors, attend Dr. King's funeral.

warned that continued riots could produce a fascist state. But let us see to it also that the conditions that cause riots are promptly removed, as the president of the United States is trying to get us to do so. Let black and white alike search their hearts; and if there be prejudice in our hearts against any racial or ethnic group, let us exterminate it and let us pray, as Martin Luther King Jr. would pray if he could: "Father, forgive them for they know not what they do." If we do this, Martin Luther King Jr. will have died a redemptive death from which all mankind will benefit…

I close by saying to you what Martin Luther King Jr. believed: If physical death was the price he had to pay to rid America of prejudice and injustice, nothing could be more redemptive. And, to paraphrase the words of the immortal John Fitzgerald Kennedy, permit me to say that Martin Luther King Jr.'s unfinished work on earth must truly be our own.

April 9, 1968
Atlanta, Georgia

A mule-drawn wagon carries the body of the martyred leader through the streets of Atlanta.

"Then my living shall not be in vain."

Excerpted from the sermon titled "The Drum Major Instinct," delivered at Ebenezer Baptist Church in Atlanta, Georgia, on February 4, 1968.

Every now and then I guess we all think realistically about that day when we will be victimized with what is life's final common denominator—that something that we call death.

We all think about it, and every now and then I think about my own death, and I think about my own funeral. And I don't think of it in a morbid sense. And every now and then I ask myself, "What is it that I would want said?" And I leave the word to you this morning.

If any of you are around when I have to meet my day, I don't want a long funeral. And if you get somebody to deliver the eulogy, tell them not to talk too long. And every now and then I wonder what I want them to say. Tell them not to mention that I have a Nobel Peace Prize—that isn't important. Tell them not to mention that I have three or four hundred other awards—that's not important. Tell them not to mention where I went to school.

I'd like somebody to mention that day that Martin Luther King, Jr., tried to give his life serving others.

I'd like for somebody to say that day that Martin Luther King, Jr., tried to love somebody.

I want you to say that day that I tried to be right on the war question.

I want you to be able to say that day that I did try to feed the hungry.

And I want you to be able to say that day that I did try in my life to clothe those who were naked.

I want you to say on that day that I did try in my life to visit those who were in prison.

I want you to say that I tried to love and serve humanity.

Yes, if you want to say that I was a drum major, say that I was a drum major for justice. Say

that I was a drum major for peace. I was a drum major for righteousness. And all of the other shallow things will not matter.

 I won't have any money to leave behind. I won't have the fine and luxurious things of life to leave behind. But I just want to leave a committed life behind. And that's all I want to say.

If I can help somebody as I pass along,

If I can cheer somebody with a word or song,

If I can show somebody he's traveling wrong,

Then my living will not be in vain.

If I can do my duty as a Christian ought,

If I can bring salvation to a world once wrought,

If I can spread the message as the master taught,

Then my living will not be in vain.

In a solemn, watchful line, striking Memphis garbagemen wear "I Am A Man" signs and declared that they were just asking for simple freedom and justice and decent salaries for their families. Their cause was supported by Dr. Martin Luther King, Jr.

The day before he was assassinated, Dr. King stands on the balcony of the Lorraine Motel in Memphis with Hosea Williams, Jesse Jackson, and Rev. Ralph D. Abernathy.

The view from the window where police say a man fired the shot that killed Dr. King.

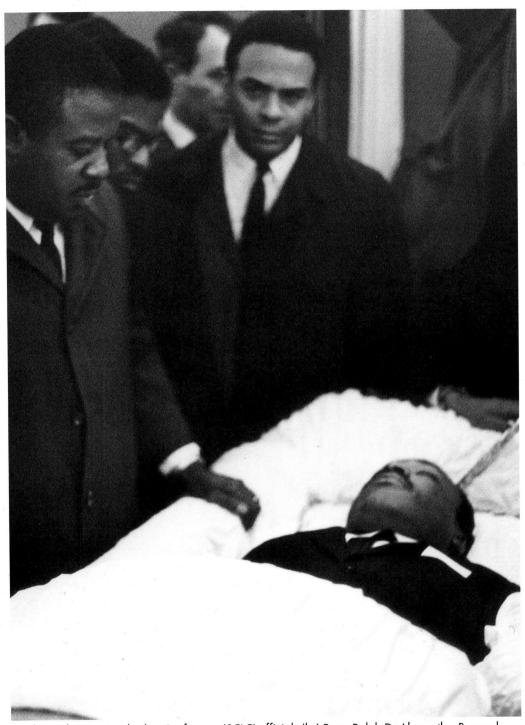

Southern Christian Leadership Conference (SCLC) officials (l-r) Revs. Ralph D. Abernathy, Bernard Lee, and Andrew Young mourn their fallen leader in Memphis.

"I would challenge you today to see that his spirit never dies and that we will go forward from this experience, which to me represents the crucifixion, on toward the resurrection and redemption of his spirit. We must carry on…"
—Coretta Scott King, April 8, 1968

Jacqueline Kennedy, widow of the assassinated President John F. Kennedy, comforts Mrs. King.

Viewing Dr. King's body with Mrs. King and her four children, Yolanda, Bernice, Martin III, and Dexter, is Robert Williams, a college professor at Grambling College (now Grambling State University), and a friend and classmate of Dr. King. He sang one of Dr. King's favorite songs at the funeral services.

EBONY Publisher John H. Johnson offers condolences to Mrs. Coretta Scott King.

EBONY Editor Lerone Bennett, Jr. (c) is joined at the services by New York Gov. Nelson D. Rockefeller and Charles Evers, brother of slain civil rights leader Medgar Evers.

April 9, 1968: Hundreds gather at Ebenezer Baptist Church in Atlanta, GA, site of Dr. King's funeral. Dignitaries include governors, senators, and other political leaders.

Bereaved celebrities proceed to Dr. King's funeral. Among them (l-r), Nancy Wilson, Eartha Kitt, Sidney Poitier, Sammy Davis, Jr., Motown founder Berry Gordy, and actor Marlon Brando.

Mrs. Lenore Romney and Michigan Gov. George W. Romney sit next to activist Dick Gregory. Seated behind them are the late President John F. Kennedy's widow Jacqueline Kennedy and his brother Senator Edward M. Kennedy (D-MA).

Fifty thousand
people walk five
miles from
Ebenezer Baptist
Church to
Morehouse
College, where
final tributes
were paid.

The U.S. and Georgia State flags fly at half-staff atop the Georgia Capitol building.

In 82-degree heat, crowds gather at Morehouse College, where Dr. Benjamin E. Mays delivered the eulogy.

21

The King Family

Martin Luther King, Jr., married Coretta Scott at her parents' home in Marion, AL on June 8, 1953. Rev. Martin L. King, Sr., (Daddy King) performed the ceremony.

Below, proud parents admire their firstborn, Yolanda Denise King.

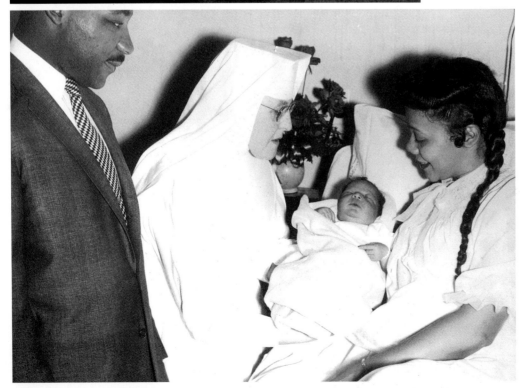

King and eldest son, Martin III, attend the World's Fair, August 12, 1964.

Dr. and Mrs. King enjoy playing with their children, Yolanda and Martin III.

"His children knew that Daddy loved them. The time he spent with them was well spent."

—Coretta King

Dr. King is welcomed with a kiss by Mrs. King after he left court in Montgomery, AL, in 1956.

Dr. and Mrs. King and their children prepare to take a family photo in their front yard.

Dr. and Mrs. King sing hymns with their eldest daughter, Yolanda.

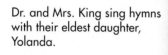

National leaders Dr. King, A. Philip Randolph and Roy Wilkins organized the May, 1957, Prayer Pilgrimage in Washington, D.C. It was the largest Black civil rights demonstration of its time.

Dr. Martin Luther King, Jr., the young pastor of Montgomery's Dexter Avenue Baptist Church, gives Mrs. King and daughter, Yolanda a smile (opposite page) and talks with members after service.

Dr. King entered Morehouse College at age fifteen and graduated in 1948 with a B.A. in sociology. In 1951, he earned a Bachelor of Divinity from Crozer Theological Seminary in Chester, PA. In 1955, Dr. King earned a Ph.D. in theology from Boston University.

King's first book, *Stride Toward Freedom: The Montgomery Story*, was published in May of 1958. While autographing copies in a Harlem department store, King was attacked and stabbed by a mentally unbalanced woman who plunged a letter opener into his chest.

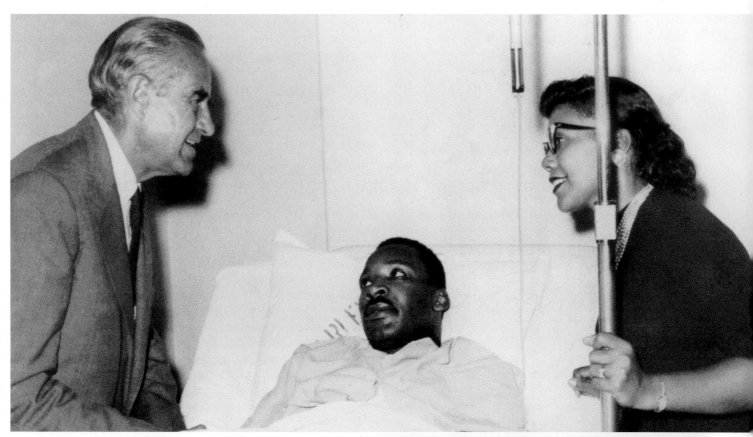

Dr. and Mrs. King talk with New York Gov. Averell Harriman in Harlem Hospital, where he was treated for the stab wound. Harriman noted that Dr. King was the only calm person in the hospital after the stabbing.

Dr. King's mother, Mrs. Alberta King and wife, Coretta, sit at his bedside following the attack.

Letter from a Birmingham jail...

Excerpts from "Letter from Birmingham Jail," written on April 18, 1963

...We know through painful experience that freedom is never voluntarily given by the oppressor, it must be demanded by the oppressed. Frankly, I have yet to engage in a direct action movement campaign that was "well-timed" in the view of those who have not suffered unduly from the disease of segregation. For years now I have heard the word "Wait!" It rings in the ear of every Negro with piercing familiarity. This "Wait" has almost always meant "Never." It has been a tranquilizing thalidomide, relieving the emotional stress for a moment only to give birth to an ill-formed infant of frustration...We have waited for more than three hundred and forty years for our constitutional and God-given rights...

Nonviolent direct action seeks to create such a crisis and foster such a tension that a community which has constantly refused to negotiate is forced to confront the issue. It seeks so to dramatize the issue that it can no longer be ignored. My citing the creation of tension as part of the work of the nonviolent register may sound rather shocking. But I must confess that I am not afraid of the word "tension." I have earnestly opposed violent tension, but there is a type of constructive, nonviolent tension which is necessary for growth...

There are two types of laws: just and unjust... I would agree with St. Augustine that "An unjust law is no law at all."...

I hope you are able to see the distinction I am trying to point out. In no sense do I advocate evading or defying the law, as would the rabid segregationist. That would lead to anarchy. One who breaks an unjust law must do so openly, lovingly... I submit that an individual who breaks a law that conscience tells him is unjust, and who willingly accepts the penalty of imprisonment in order to arouse the conscience of the community over its injustice, is in reality expressing the highest respect for law...

Dr. King expresses his frustration at the treatment of demonstrators in Birmingham.

Young student demonstrators try to help one another as they are attacked with water hoses.

I began thinking about the fact that I stand in the middle of two opposing forces in the Negro community. One is a force of complacency made up in part of Negroes who, as a result of long years of oppression, are so drained of self-respect and a sense of "somebodiness" that they have adjusted to segregation; and in part of a few middle-class Negroes who, because of a degree of academic and economic security and because in some ways they profit by segregation, have become insensitive to the problems of the masses. The other force is one of bitterness and hatred, and it comes perilously close to advocating violence…

I have tried to stand between these two forces, saying that we need emulate neither the "do nothingism" of the complacent nor the hatred and despair of the black nationalist. For there is the more excellent way of love and nonviolent protest. I am grateful to God that, through the influence of the Negro church, the way of nonviolence became an integral part of our struggle.

If this philosophy had not emerged, by now many streets of the South would, I am convinced, be flowing with blood. And I am further convinced that if our white brothers dismiss as "rabble rousers" and "outside agitators" those of us who employ nonviolent direct action, and if they refuse to support our nonviolent efforts, millions of Negroes will, out of frustration and despair, seek solace and security in black nationalist ideologies—a development that would inevitably lead to a frightening racial nightmare…

So the question is not whether we will be extremists, but what kind of extremists will we be? Will we be extremists for hate or for love? Will we be extremists for the preservation of injustice or for the extension of justice?… Jesus Christ was an extremist for love, truth, and goodness…Perhaps the South, the nation and the world are in dire need of creative extremists…

In Albany, GA, during his 1961–1962 anti-segregation campaign, Dr. King was jailed four times. Demonstrators held prayer vigils, one of which led to their arrests.

Workers and students wait for rides in cars rather than ride on buses during the Montgomery Bus Boycott.

In Montgomery, AL, on Dec. 1, 1955, Mrs. Rosa Parks was arrested for refusing to give up her seat on a bus to a white man. Dr. King, the young, new minister at Dexter Avenue Baptist Church, joined community leaders in organizing a one-day bus boycott that lasted 382 days. On Nov. 13, 1956, the Supreme Court ruled that segregation on buses was unconstitutional, and the bus boycott was called off.

In the twelve years of nonviolent struggle for human rights and freedom that followed the bus boycott, Dr. King grew as an orator, organizer, writer, and philosopher, but he never abandoned his principles of peace and love.

More than 250,000 people participated in the March on Washington, D.C., August 28, 1963. They came by plane, bus, train, and on foot, and from every walk of life.

Odetta (below, l), folksinger and musician, performed at the March on Washington. Entertainer Josephine Baker (below, r) flew in from Paris for the historic demonstration.

(Above) Dr. King and other civil rights leaders confer with President John F. Kennedy at the White House.

(Below) Sharing a moment at the March on Washington are (l-r) actor Charlton Heston, author James Baldwin, actor Marlon Brando and Dr. King's close confidant, entertainer and activist Harry Belafonte.

Activist, author, and comedian Dick Gregory speaks to marchers during the event.

Daisy Bates (l), mentor for the Little Rock Nine, and Rosa Parks (r) at the March on Washington.

The March on Washington was the largest peaceful demonstration for civil rights in history.

"I have a dream..."

Excerpts from the "I Have a Dream" address, delivered at the March on Washington for Jobs and Freedom on August 28, 1963

Fivescore years ago, a great American, in whose symbolic shadow we stand today, signed the Emancipation Proclamation. This momentous decree came as a great beacon light of hope to millions of Negro slaves who had been seared in the flames of withering injustice. It came as a joyous daybreak to end the long night of their captivity.

But one hundred years later, the Negro is still not free. One hundred years later, the life of the Negro is still sadly crippled by the manacles of segregation and the chains of discrimination. One hundred years later, the Negro lives on a lonely island of poverty in the midst of a vast ocean of material prosperity. One hundred years later, the Negro is still languished in the corners of American society and finds himself an exile in his own land…

There will be neither rest nor tranquility in America until the Negro is granted his citizenship rights. The whirlwinds of revolt will continue to shake the foundations of our nation until the bright day of justice emerges…

I say to you today, my friends, so even though we face the difficulties of today and tomorrow, I still have a dream. It is a dream deeply rooted in the American dream.

I have a dream that one day this nation will rise up and live out the true meaning of its creed; "We hold these truths to be self-evident; that all men are created equal."

I have a dream that one day on the red hills of Georgia the sons of former slaves and the sons of former slave owners will be able to sit down together at the table of brotherhood.

I have a dream that one day even the state of Mississippi, a state sweltering with the heat of injustice, sweltering with the heat of oppression, will be transformed into an oasis of freedom and justice.

I have a dream that my four little children will one day live in a nation where they will not be judged by the color of their skin but by the content of their character.

I have a dream today.

I have a dream that one day down in Alabama, with its vicious racists, with its governor having his lips dripping with the words of interposition and nullification, one day right there in Alabama little black boys and black girls will be able to join hands with little white boys and white girls as sisters and brothers.

I have a dream today.

I have a dream that one day every valley shall be exalted, and every hill and mountain shall be made low, the rough places will be made plain, and the crooked places will be made straight, and the glory of the Lord shall be revealed, and all flesh shall see it together.

This is our hope. This is the faith that I go back to the South with. With this faith we will be able to hew out of the mountain of despair a stone of hope. With this faith we will be able to transform the jangling discords of our nation into a beautiful symphony of brotherhood. With this faith

we will be able to work together, to pray together, to struggle together…knowing that we will be free one day…This will be the day…when all of God's children will be able to sing with new meaning:

My country 'tis of thee, sweet land of liberty, of thee I sing.
Land where my fathers died, land of the pilgrim's pride,
from every mountain side, let freedom ring.

And if America is to be a great nation this must come true.

And so let freedom ring from the prodigious hilltops of New Hampshire.

Let freedom ring from the mighty mountains of New York.

Let freedom ring from the heightening Alleghenies of Pennsylvania.

Let freedom ring from the snowcapped Rockies of Colorado…

Let freedom ring from every hill and molehill of Mississippi.

 From every mountainside, let freedom ring.

And when this happens, when we allow freedom [to] ring, when we let it ring from every village and every hamlet, from every state and every city, we will be able to speed up that day when all of God's children, black men and white men, Jews and Gentiles, Protestants and Catholics, will be able to join hands and sing, in the words of the old Negro spiritual,

"Free at last! Free at last!
Thank God Almighty, we are free at last!"

August 28, 1963
Washington, D.C.

Dr. Martin Luther King, Jr., made many journeys. In India, he said, he came as a pilgrim.

During one visit to India, Dr. and Mrs. King met with the Prime Minister of the Republic of India, Jawaharlal Nehru.

Mrs. Coretta Scott King sings during a visit to India. She graduated from the New England Conservatory of Music in 1954 with a major in Voice and a minor in Violin.

Rev. Martin Luther King, Jr. and Rev. Ralph D. Abernathy visit Monsignor Paul Marcinkus and Pope Paul VI at the Vatican on September 18, 1964.

Dr. King stands with Willy Brandt, the mayor of West Berlin, during a visit to the Berlin Wall. Dr. King was the principal speaker at the opening of the 1964 West Berlin Festival.

Dr. King (r), stands with his interpreter as he preaches in East Berlin. Dr. King preached on both sides of the Berlin Wall.

In 1964, during his trip to Oslo to receive the Nobel Peace Prize, Dr. King was greeted with a round of receptions, luncheons, and formal dinners. Dr. and Mrs. King (above) share a moment before attending an affair at the Grand Hotel. Dr. King is shown in tails, and Mrs. King wore a floor-length silk melon-colored gown with a beaded jacket.

Queen Louise of Sweden (above, r) congratulates the Nobel Laureate.

Dr. King shakes the hand of King Olav V, of Norway. On the morning of the Nobel ceremony, King Olav V sent his personal limousine to bring Dr. and Mrs. King to his Royal Palace for a 30-minute audience. King Olav V usually met with dignitaries for only 10 minutes.

(Opposite page) Dr. and Mrs. King celebrate privately with family in Oslo following the ceremony. They are (standing, l-r) his mother, Alberta King, father Rev. Martin L. King, Sr., sister, Christina Farris, and brother, Rev. A.D. King.

The brutality demonstrators faced during the 1965 "March on Ballot Boxes" in Selma, AL, was televised across the nation. People from all over the country, including many clergymen, came to protest the violence and support the demonstrators.

Dr. Martin Luther King, Jr., led 25,000 civil rights marchers to the state Capitol in Montgomery, AL, from March 21–25, 1965, to protest the denial of voting rights to blacks. Participating in the 54-mile march from Selma to Montgomery were Dr. King and his wife Coretta Scott King, Rev. Ralph D. Abernathy and his wife Juanita, Nobel Peace Prize-winner Dr. Ralph Bunche, and Dick Gregory. The marchers walked 12 miles a day and slept in fields. They also sang freedom songs along the way and at each stop were greeted by supporters. At the conclusion of the 5-day march through Alabama, an estimated 50,000 well-wishers from every state in the country gathered at the foot of the state Capitol and celebrated the grand event.

The Selma to Montgomery March was a victory over segregation forces and Gov. George Wallace, but the triumph gave way to grief when two of the people who had helped to transport the marchers, Mrs. Viola Liuzzo and Leroy Moton, were shot at by the Ku Klux Klan. Mrs. Liuzzo was killed.

Undaunted, although drenched, Dr. Martin Luther King sings out vigorously with Alabama marchers who meet the downpour with uplifted spirits. Mrs. Coretta King, protected only by an umbrella and a raincap, joins her husband in leading the song.

In Montgomery, Alabama

Excerpts from a speech titled "Our God is Marching On!" delivered at the state Capitol building in Montgomery, Alabama, on March 25, 1965

…Last Sunday, more than eight thousand of us started on a mighty walk from Selma, Alabama. …We have walked on meandering highways and rested our bodies on rocky byways. Some of our faces are burned from the outpourings of the sweltering sun. Some have literally slept in the mud. We have been drenched by the rains. Our bodies are tired and our feet are somewhat sore.

But today as I stand before you and think back over that great march, I can say, as Sister Pollard said—a seventy-year-old Negro woman who lived in this community during the bus boycott—and one day, she was asked while walking if she didn't want to ride. And when she answered, "No," the person said, "Well, aren't you tired?" And with her ungrammatical profundity, she said, "My feets is tired, but my soul is rested." And in a real sense this afternoon, we can say that our feet are tired, but our souls are rested.

They told us we wouldn't get here. And there were those who said that we would get here only over their dead bodies, but all the world today knows that we are here and we are standing before the forces of power in the state of Alabama saying, "We ain't goin' let nobody turn us around."

There never was a moment in American history more honorable and more inspiring than the pilgrimage of clergymen and laymen of every race and faith pouring into Selma to face danger at the side of its embattled Negroes.

Our whole campaign in Alabama has been centered around the right to vote. In focusing the attention of the nation and the world today on the flagrant denial of the right to vote, we are exposing the very origin, the root cause, of racial segregation in the Southland…

Toward the end of the Reconstruction era, something very significant happened. That is what was known as the Populist Movement. The leaders of this movement began…uniting the Negro and white masses into a voting bloc that threatened to drive the Bourbon interests from the command posts of political power in the South…

Thus, the threat of the free exercise of the ballot by the Negro and the white masses alike resulted in the establishment of a segregated society. They segregated Southern money from the poor whites; they segregated southern mores from the rich whites; they segregated Southern churches from Christianity; they segregated Southern minds from honest thinking; and they segregated the Negro from everything…

We've come a long way since that travesty of justice was perpetrated upon the American mind…

Today I want to tell the city of Selma, today I want to say to the state of Alabama, today I want to say to the people of America and the nations of the world, that we are not about to turn around. We are on the move now.

Yes, we are on the move and no wave of racism can stop us. We are on the move now. The burning of our churches will not deter us. The bombing of our homes will not dissuade us. We are on the move now. The beating and killing of our clergymen and young people will not divert us. We are on the move now. The wanton release of their known murderers would not discourage us. We are on the move now…

Let us therefore continue our triumphant march…Let us march on segregated housing…Let us march on segregated schools…Let us march on poverty…Let us march on ballot boxes…

My people, my people, listen. The battle is in our hands…

I know you are asking today, "How long will it take?"…I come to say to you this afternoon, however difficult the moment, however frustrating the hour, it will not be long, because truth crushed to earth will rise again.

How long? Not long, because no lie can live forever.

How long? Not long, because you shall reap what you sow…

How long? Not long, because the arc of the moral universe is long, but it bends toward justice.

How long? Not long, because:

Mine eyes have seen the glory of the coming of the Lord;
He is trampling out the vintage where the grapes of wrath are stored;
He has loosed the fateful lightning of his terrible swift sword;
His truth is marching on.
He has sounded forth the trumpet that shall never call retreat;
He is sifting out the hearts of men before His judgment seat.
O, be swift, my soul, to answer Him! Be jubilant my feet!
Our God is marching on…

President John F. Kennedy and President Lyndon B. Johnson were both moved by Dr. King's campaigns and dynamic leadership. The Civil Rights Bill of 1964, which prohibited discrimination in employment, was passed in a mood of reparation and remorse after Kennedy's assassination. The Civil Rights Bill of 1968, banning racial discrimination in the housing market, was signed the week after Dr. Martin Luther King, Jr., was assassinated in Memphis, TN.

Dr. King and President Lyndon B. Johnson listen to a report on the status of civil rights during a White House meeting in 1964.

On June 23, 1963, Dr. King led 125,000 people in a freedom walk in Detroit, where he first shared the sentiments of his "I Have a Dream" speech.

James Meredith, the lone student to integrate the University of Mississippi in 1962, graduated on August 18, 1963. He started an even lonelier pilgrimage from Memphis to Jackson in June of 1966 to encourage voter registration. He was shot and wounded by a sniper, but was able to rejoin the march in its last stage.

Marching in Mississippi are SCLC leaders Hosea Williams, Bernard Lee, Dr. King, and Student Non-Violent Coordinating Committee (SNCC) leaders Stokely Carmichael and Willie Rick.

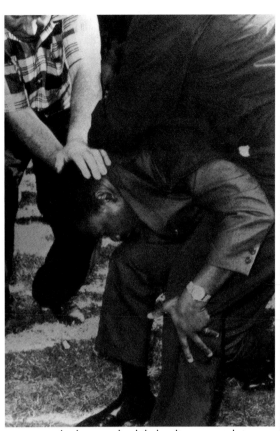

Dr. King is hit by a rock while leading a march in Chicago.

As part of the Chicago Freedom Movement, Dr. King targeted discrimination in housing and labor in the North. He moved into a property on the West Side of Chicago in 1966 and held rallies, marches, and demonstrations to highlight the inequities nationally.

Dr. King speaks at a grassroots meeting in a West Side Chicago neighborhood.

Dr. King is seen marching with supporters in downtown Chicago.

Harry Belafonte and renowned gospel singer Mahalia Jackson join Dr. King at the Chicago Freedom Festival, a part of the Chicago Freedom Movement.

On stage at the Chicago Freedom Festival with Dr. King and Mahalia Jackson are (l-r) Sidney Poitier, Harry Belafonte, Dick Gregory, Liz Lands, and Al Raby.

Dr. King addresses a crowd of more than 50,000 supporters at Chicago's Soldier Field.

Dr. King speaks at a press conference with Chicago leaders.

Rev. Jesse Jackson (l) and Dr. King confer with Cirilo McSween, national treasurer of SCLC.

During the Chicago Freedom Movement of 1966 Dr. King captures the attention of over 10,000 at the International Amphitheater during the Chicago Freedom Festival.

Pictures of Dr. King at play are rare because there were few off-duty hours, but the impassioned speaker and dedicated worker for humanity enjoyed being a husband and father.

Dr. King (l) enjoys a game of softball with his aides.

Dr. King (r) demonstrates his skills at the pool table as Chicago teens look on in awe.

King worked on his last book, *Where Do We Go From Here: Chaos or Community?* in Ocho Rios, Jamaica, and enjoyed a three-week escape from the headlines.

Dr. King is seen marching with Dr. Benjamin Spock during a protest against the Vietnam War. Dr. King's conscience spoke to him about war as clearly as it spoke to him about civil rights.

CHILDREN ARE NOT BORN TO BURN

R NOW!

Dr. and Mrs. King share affection as he departs for a trip in 1965. They were married only 14 years and 10 months. After his death, Mrs. King spent the next 38 years working to fulfill his legacy before she died on January 31, 2006.

Dr. Martin Luther King, Jr., makes his last speech in Memphis supporting a strike by sanitation workers.

"I've seen the promised land."

Excerpt from Dr. King's last sermon, "I've Been to the Mountaintop," delivered on April 3, 1968 in Memphis, Tennessee.

I don't know what will happen now; we've have got some difficult days ahead. But it really doesn't matter with me now, because I've been to the mountaintop…Like anybody, I would like to live a long life…But I'm not concerned about that now. I just want to do God's will. And He has allowed me to go up to the mountain…I've seen the promised land. I may not get there with you, but I want you to know tonight that we, as a people, will get to the promised land. And so I'm happy tonight; I'm not worried about anything; I'm not fearing any man. "Mine eyes have seen the glory of the coming of the Lord."

The Nobel Peace Prize was presented to Dr. Martin Luther King, Jr., on December 10, 1964. At the time, Dr. King, 35, was the youngest person to receive the award. Standing amid banks of 1,000 freshly-cut white carnations, Dr. King accepts the Nobel gold medal and scroll from Nobel committee director Gunnar Jahn. Dr. King also received a check for 273,000 svenske kroner—about $54,000. Dr. King donated the money to civil rights work in the United States.

Not only in his acceptance speech, but in every press conference and in each of his numerous appearances on European radio and TV, Dr. King emphasized his refusal to accept the Nobel award as "an honor to me personally." He insisted he was "only a trustee, accepting this prize on behalf of the millions of black men, women and children, and the white people of good will, who work for freedom in the U.S. and to whom I owe all that I may be today."